*The Story of the*
# 1917 Halifax Explosion
*& The*
# Boston Tree

*Suzanne Pasternak*

◆ FriesenPress

Suite 300 - 990 Fort St
Victoria, BC, V8V 3K2
Canada

www.friesenpress.com

**Copyright © 2017 by Suzanne Pasternak**
First Edition — 2017

Illustrator: Hayden Maynard

All rights reserved.

No part of this publication may be reproduced in any form, or by any means, electronic or mechanical, including photocopying, recording, or any information browsing, storage, or retrieval system, without permission in writing from FriesenPress.

ISBN
978-1-5255-0182-1 (Hardcover)
978-1-5255-0183-8 (Paperback)
978-1-5255-0184-5 (eBook)

1. HISTORY

Distributed to the trade by The Ingram Book Company

"The Evidence is clear that in the direst of circumstances humans go to the assistance of others. That is the story told here. This is a story of heroism and gratitude in the context of the largest man made explosion in human history before World War 2. This was an explosion that reduced a good portion of the city of Halifax to rubble and killed or injured thousands of its citizens.

Suzanne Pasternak has written a compelling and compassionate story about the Halifax explosion of 1917 and the long tradition of gratitude it set in motion. It is important that in these times to be reminded that humanity embodies rich reservoirs of goodness and kindness and the spirit to do the right thing. Read it aloud, and read it again and share it widely. It is a story for all ages."

Craig Jones PhD

# Introduction

We often see how a disaster or a tragic event can bring out the best in people. Our province saw a shining example of that when something terrible happened in our capital city of Halifax back in 1917.

On the morning of December 6 that year, two ships collided in Halifax Harbour. It caused an explosion that devastated the city and surrounding area.

At that time, it was the largest man-made explosion the world had ever seen. Sadly, about 2,000 people died, and 9,000 more were hurt. The force of the blast flattened homes, and shattered glass even kilometres [miles] away. The city needed help. Doctors, firefighters and rescuers came from all over Nova Scotia, other parts of Canada…..and many came from Boston.

People there learned of the explosion that very morning. Just hours later, a train carrying doctors, nurses, and medical supplies was fighting its way through a blizzard to our city, more than 1,000 kilometres [621 miles] away.

The care, support and relief they provided helped save the lives of many who had been hurt. As you'll read in this story, they were heroes.

Bostonians and others from New England were part of the relief effort for months, sending workers, supplies and raising money to help Halifax recover.

It's now a tradition for us to say thank you each year by sending one of our fine Christmas trees to the City of Boston.

Nova Scotia had ties with the City of Boston and State of Massachusetts well before the explosion. The assistance that came afterward only made the bond between us stronger, and we want our friendship to continue.

We are so grateful for the help that was provided in our time of need. And we are so pleased to send a Christmas tree to Boston each year in gratitude and friendship, and see the warm reception it receives year after year.

I hope you enjoy this story, and learn a bit about why we are still saying thank you to Boston so many years later.

The Honourable Stephen McNeil, Premier of Nova Scotia

# *Forward*

In the early part of 2014, I was doing some research on a project I was developing about World War I and the 1917 Halifax Explosion. I came across an interesting book: a compilation of eye-witness accounts, doctor's reports, government documents, and military reports. This book had been compiled and edited by artist Graham Metson. In this compilation, there was one very long government document that I had only just begun to read when I realized its importance. This government document was written for the governor of Massachusetts, Samuel McCall, by Abraham C. Ratshesky. It read like the heart-wrenching, heart-pounding script for some Hollywood movie. I fell instantly in love with the writer, Abraham Ratshesky. He was so sincere, and had obviously been profoundly moved by what he had witnessed in Halifax after the 1917 explosion. He was Commissioner in Charge of that epic humanitarian mission, which set out from the United States to Canada within hours of the disaster.

I then went on an investigative journey to find more details about the rescue mission. Archival research in two countries, as well as Internet research, ensued. This journey eventually led me to introduce myself and this book to the relatives of Abraham Ratshesky in Boston. I subsequently dropped my other project to tell this incredible story: the real reason why Nova Scotians send a fifty-foot Christmas tree to Boston every year.

This is the story of the Massachusetts-Halifax Relief Expedition of 1917 and the ever-faithful gratitude of the city of Halifax.

# About Abraham C. Ratshesky

Ratshesky was born to immigrants in Boston in 1866.

He was a banker, politician, and diplomat, but above all he was a humanitarian, a philanthropist, and a social activist. He devoted his life to the welfare of others. His legacy lives on today in the A.C. Ratshesky Foundation, which he created in 1916. This foundation supports programs that work toward the self-sufficiency of economically disadvantaged individuals and families. Funding priority is given to the following fields of interest: family partnering in early education, employment and self-sufficiency, and active learning for preteens and teens. The Board of Trustees are descended from Abraham "Cap" Ratshesky.

"In Praise of Abraham C. Ratshesky"

This is a letter from 17-year-old Harold Walter Hoganson of Halifax to 16-year-old Harold Kennedy of Stoughton, Massachusetts. The young Hoganson boy lost three members of his family in the explosion.

"Dear Harold,

The day after the explosion, the work of relief started and thank God the noble people of Massachusetts stood by us the same as ever, ready to help us. I tell you, I don't know what we would have done without the Americans, because we were left so powerless after the explosion.

Well, the work of relief started. Buildings were put into shape for the injured and the homeless, and a man whose name will always stand sacred in every Canadian's mind is Abraham Ratshesky, the hero of dear Halifax."

# Dedication

This book is dedicated to Abraham "Cap" Ratshesky, Commissioner in Charge of the Massachusetts-Halifax Relief Expedition of 1917, Governor Samuel McCall of the state of Massachusetts, and to the personnel on that train whose brave action saved so many lives in Halifax.

### Surgeons and Doctors [All members of the Massachusetts State Guard]

Major Harold Giddings [in command]

Major A. Supple

Major Donald V. Baker [Surgeon in Chief]

Major George W. Morse

Major Peter Owen Shea

Captain Edward F. Murphy

Captain Thomas F. Harrington [Physician in Chief]

Captain John W. Dewis

Captain Robert G. Loring [Opthamologist]

Captain DeWitt G. Wilcox

Captain Nathaniel N. Morse [Anaesthetist]

Quartermasters Dept., Captain Benjamin D. Hyde

Quartermasters Dept., Captain Henry G. Lapham

*Nurses*

Miss Elizabeth Peden [in charge]

Miss Charlott Naismith

Miss Marion Nevens

Miss Mary A. Davidson

Miss Caroline E. Carlton

Miss Nellie P. Black

Miss Edith F. Perkins

Miss Elizabeth Choate

Miss Jesse McInnes

*Red Cross Representatives*

John F. Moors, Chairman, Civilian Relief Committee

C.C. Carsten, Secretary Civilian Relief Committee

Miss Katherine McMahon, Associate Director, Civilian Relief Committee

J. Prentice Murphy, Secretary, Children's Aid Society

Wm. H. Pear, The Boston Provident Association

Miss Marion Rowe, The Boston Associated Charities

*The Press*

A.J. Philpott, Boston Globe

R.W. Simpson, Associated Press

Roy Atkinson, Boston Post

Richard W. Sears, Boston American

J.V. Keating, Boston Herald

# Acknowledgements

My thanks to the Honorable Stephen McNeil, Premier of Nova Scotia, Press Secretary David Jackson, and Stacey Jones-Oxner, Director of Events, Communities, Culture, and Heritage for the Government of Nova Scotia, for their contributions to this book.

I will be forever grateful for the financial and editorial help given to me by Dan Dearborn. Dan is a true patron of the arts.

I thank Bev Coles, Glen Fast, Lynne Underhill, and Melanie Dugan for countless hours of editing, proofreading, and advising.

Hats off to songwriters Mark Despault and Tom Leighton, for the song "We Will See You Through".

"Bravo" to Hayden Maynard, illustrator.

# *Prologue*

A devastating explosion in the city of Halifax, Nova Scotia, in 1917, set in motion an epic humanitarian rescue mission by Governor Samuel McCall of the state of Massachusetts and Boston businessman and philanthropist Abraham Ratshesky.

And now, a century after the disaster, a yearly gesture of thanks arrives in Boston on a flatbed truck, after its 621 mile [1,000 kph] journey up the east coast from Halifax. Every year somewhere in Nova Scotia, a fifty-foot Christmas tree is carefully selected and cut down with great ceremony. This process of selecting the perfect tree and the subsequent ceremonies, as it travels through Nova Scotia and the Maritimes, pays homage to the 1917 tragedy. This tragedy changed the lives of so many, and its impact is deeply rooted in the collective memory of the city of Halifax forever.

Throughout the year, folks from across the province contact the Nova Scotia Department of Natural Resources to find out if they have a fifty-foot Balsam Fir or a red or white Spruce that they would like to donate for Boston. The members of the Department of Natural Resources will travel anywhere in the province in order to see the tree and meet the owners. When the perfect tree is finally found, it is cut down and sent on its very special diplomatic mission.

This tree stands on the Boston Commons in front of the state house, and its lighting is a major celebration in Boston. This Christmas tree stands as a symbol of peace on earth and good will to all of humanity. In particular, it is a symbol of the friendship that exists between two great nations: Canada and the United States.

Every December, 30,000 people attend the lighting of the tree, and another 300,000 watch it on television.

This is the true, inspiring story behind the Boston Christmas Tree:

# *Chapter 1*

**December 6, 1917**
**Halifax, Nova Scotia**
**8:43 a.m.**

It was an unusually warm winter day with a clear blue sky and sunlight dancing on the water in Halifax harbor. School children were walking down the street on their way to school. Mothers were beginning the chores for the day, taking advantage of the warm sunshine and gentle breeze to hang out the laundry. World War I was still raging in Europe, and many of the husbands, brothers, fathers, and sons were away fighting the war. That morning, women and children eagerly waited for the sight of the postman bringing them letters from their loved ones. The good people of Halifax were thoroughly enjoying this unexpectedly spring-like morning. Normally at this time of year, they would be bracing themselves against the cold, wild winds that swept in from the Atlantic Ocean.

For those in the city who had a view of Halifax Harbor, there was a bit of excitement going on. The harbor had been extremely busy since the beginning of World War I, three years earlier. Ships from all over the world were coming and going, carrying supplies, ammunition, medical supplies, and the like back and forth across the Atlantic to Europe. But this morning there was something more. One by one, and then in groups, people noticed something strange out in the harbor. Smoke was rising from a ship. There was more smoke than was normally seen from the many stacks moving up and down the harbor. Then flames became apparent and very visible. Fierce red flames seemed to shoot straight up into the sky, creating a spectacular column of black smoke. Curious, many stood at their living-room windows to watch the fire, or else went out into the street to watch. People thought that it was an oil tanker on fire. The ship was clearly drifting toward the Halifax shore.

Constant Upham stood watching the fire burning aboard the ship, and quickly realized how serious it was. Upham owned a general store and was the only resident in the neighborhood who owned a telephone. He proceeded to call all the fire halls in the area, including West Street, Brunswick Street, Gottingen Street, and Quinpool Road. Meanwhile the firemen from the north end responded to the alarm that had been pulled on the dock. There was an assumption at first that this was a regular fire, started by burning embers that were dumped from a ship's boiler. When they arrived on the scene, they realized that it was a ship on fire, and that the heat was so intense they could hardly look at it, let alone get anywhere near it. To the firefighters, it appeared that two ships had collided, sparking an intensive and out-of-control blaze aboard one of the vessels. Captain Condon pulled the Box 83 alarm for the second time, which signaled that they needed more backup immediately.

In fact, at 8:43 a.m., the Norwegian supply ship *Imo* had collided with the side of the French ship *Mont Blanc,* showering her deck with sparks. Due to wartime military security measures, it was not common knowledge that the *Mont Blanc* was carrying 2,300 tons (2.09 million kg) of highly explosive Picric Acid, 61 tons (55,339 kg) of highly explosive gun-cotton, steeped in nitric and sulphuric acid, 225 tons (204,120 kg) of TNT dynamite, and on deck, 246 tons (223,170 kg) of highly flammable benzol. The benzol was stored in barrels, which were jostled loose from their containment during the collision. It poured out of several barrels onto the deck and ignited. The fire quickly grew large and out of control. The *Mont Blanc* crew were well aware of the deadly cargo they carried. They immediately realized that there was no way to get the fire under control, and abandoned the ship. In a state of panic, they jumped into two lifeboats and rowed for their lives to the shore opposite the one their unmanned ship was now drifting toward.

The fire on deck spread rapidly to the lower levels and heated the chemicals and explosives stored below to a critical temperature. Onlookers throughout the north end of the city, as well as firefighters and police, were tragically unaware of the danger they were in.

Meanwhile, on Pier six, dispatcher Vincent Coleman had arrived to work after kissing his young wife and small child goodbye. Unknowingly, that would be their last kiss and a tragic final goodbye.

Coleman was responsible for controlling train-traffic in and out of the busy Halifax Harbor. Because it was wartime, the amount of traffic, both by land and sea, had drastically increased. Shortly after arriving to work, an eerie, metallic, groaning sound echoed over the harbor. Coleman looked out the window to see black smoke and flames shooting into the sky from the deck of the *Mont Blanc*. Several minutes later, a sailor came crashing through the door into the office. He was one of the few people who knew that the *Mont Blanc* was carrying such a lethal cargo. In a state of panic, he warned Coleman and his boss to run for their lives, because the *Mont Blanc* was carrying tons of ammunition that was about to explode.

As the men began to run from the pier, Coleman remembered that, at 8:55 a.m., a train-load of over 300 passengers was due to arrive, passing right in front of the ship of fire. Disregarding his own safety, he ran back to his office and sent out a telegram: "Stop the train. Ammunition ship on fire in harbor heading for pier six, Goodbye." Sending that telegram, and saving that train, was the last duty ever to be performed by Coleman.

The Story of the 1917 Halifax Explosion and the Boston Tree

When the fire, both above and below deck, heated the other stored chemicals to a critical temperature, detonation occurred, resulting in a massive explosion at 9:06 a.m., which shredded the *Mont Blanc* and sent fire and white-hot shrapnel in all directions at tremendous speed. The earth shook beneath those on shore, as a shock-wave moved through the earth at 13,000 miles per hour (20,920 kph), followed by the horrific shock-wave above ground. In a heartbeat, 2,000 people lay dead and 9,000 were critically wounded.

**Then all communication into and out of the city of Halifax ceased.**

# Chapter 2

**Boston, Massachusetts, two hours later**
**11:00 a.m.**

Governor Samuel McCall had arrived at his office in the state building early in the morning, to get caught up on some paperwork. He was on the phone with a colleague, leaning back in his leather chair and gazing out his window at the bright blue sky, when his aide suddenly came bursting into his office.

Breathlessly, he motioned to the governor to end the phone conversation. When McCall hung up the phone, the aide said, "Sorry, sir, but we received a message from the train dispatcher in Halifax. It said, 'Stop all trains. Munition ship on fire in harbor heading for pier six. Goodbye.' After that, sir, we have been unable to contact anybody in Halifax. We have tried telegraph and phones, and we cannot contact a soul! All communications with Halifax have gone silent."

The governor told the aide to send a telegram to the mayor of Halifax. They received no response. "Get a hold of the War and Navy Department in Washington D.C., to see if they know anything," McCall told him.

The aide did as he was directed and then returned, saying, "Sir, Washington knows nothing, but they will send a wireless message along the coast through the navy, and try to reach the mayor of Halifax."

But there was no response to the wireless message sent by the U.S. Navy. Governor McCall called his trusted friend, the Honorable Abraham Ratshesky, and told him he was going to assemble an emergency committee. He told Ratshesky that a disaster of some sort had occurred in Halifax and that a plan was needed to get relief there as soon as possible.

In a few hours, Ratshesky called the governor back. "Samuel," he said, "I spoke with Colonel William Brooks, Acting Surgeon General for the state, and if we can get a train right away, he could have a team of surgeons, doctors, and nurses, as well as medical supplies, organized within hours."

"Excellent!" said the governor.

"Leave this with me," Ratshesky said. "I will make sure we get that train! Also Samuel, I have heard from the American Red Cross seeking permission to send seven representatives on the train with us. I agreed without your permission. I hope that's all right with you."

"Yes, of course," the governor replied. "From this point forward, you are the Commissioner in Charge of this train."

The doctors involved were all military-trained officers. They were familiar with battlefield triage, search and rescue, and emergency medicine. The American Red Cross had learned a lot about emergency response after the devastating San Francisco earth quake of 1906, which had left thousands injured, killed, and homeless. Since they did not know what had happened in Halifax, they automatically put emergency-preparedness plans in place.

By 10:00 that night, Ratshesky called the governor. "Samuel, we are ready to pull out of the train station now."

"Excellent work, Abraham, and God bless you all on this mission. Please call or wire me from every station stop along the way."

Ratshesky stayed up all night. Thousands of ideas and possible plans were burning through his mind. The train at last crossed the border into Canada. At every stop, he wired a message to the mayor of Halifax, but there was never any response. At every station where they stopped, more rumors began to surface. The closer they got to Nova Scotia, the more terrifying the rumors became. It became clear that there had been a terrific explosion that had caused windows to explode across the city and that a very high percentage of the population were badly burned.

Ratshesky began to realize that they had too few supplies and staff to handle the number and severity of injuries he now anticipated. He needed to get word to Boston and get them to send not only more medical relief but also building materials—mainly glass and putty. If windows had been blown-out across the city, they would have to act quickly to repair them to keep out the snow and cold for the survivors.

When the train reached St. John, New Brunswick, those on the train got the first real taste of the horror, hearing eye-witness accounts of the destruction. They also learned that most telephone and telegraph wires were down around the city. It was at around this time that the vicious snowstorm, which would threaten the rescue efforts, began.

Ratshesky wired the governor. "Samuel, things are going from bad to worse here. We are in St. John, New Brunswick and have been caught in a blizzard. From Boston, send a train-load of glass, putty, and building supplies of all kinds. Send another train-load of medical supplies and personnel immediately. The good people of St. John, God bless them, have come forward with a considerable amount of medical supplies. At every stop, we are overwhelmed by doctors and nurses wanting to come aboard. Every available space is now filled."

The severity of the storm increased, and the train lost a lot of time between St. John and Moncton. Then disaster struck: The train's engine broke down, coming to a lurching halt that woke many of the sleeping relief workers. Despair sped through the train. It quickly became cold inside the cars, and the gale-force winds made a haunting moaning sound as it swirled around the train. It took several hours to repair the engine. Ratshesky encouraged the relief teams to try to get some sleep. He reminded them that, once they got into the devastated city, they would hit the ground running and not have time to sleep, probably for days on end. Unfortunately, even once the engines were repaired, it was discovered that the train had lost a lot of its power and ran much more slowly.

As they tried to cross Folley Mountain, they encountered another disastrous obstacle: an impassable snowdrift that lay across the tracks. The conductor of the train told Ratshesky that they could go no farther. Ratshesky refused to accept this. He showed the conductor his orders, which specifically stated that this special train had the right of way.

Ratshesky pleaded with the railroad men to do everything in their power to clear the track. He refused to take no for an answer. "The people of Halifax are in desperate trouble tonight. There are what sounds like thousands of casualties caught in this snowstorm, in the dark and without hope. We will get there tonight, and our doctors and nurses, along with other doctors and nurses from nearby Canadian cities, will stay on the job until the homeless and hurt can see daylight again. Please clear this track now, gentlemen!"

The men recognized that the situation was tremendously urgent and every minute was precious. Into the darkness of the storm they went, climbing onto the massive snowdrift with lanterns and shovels. They worked like Trojans, shoveling for a solid hour, as steam was discharged in blasts from the train's engines to erode the towering mountains of snow, which rose higher than the door of the baggage car. Finally, the train's own power was able to break them through, backing up, gaining as much forward momentum as possible, and then ploughing through the drift, amidst great cheers from all on board.

At 3:00 a.m., December 8, the train arrived in Halifax—just thirty hours after disaster had struck. There were sixty-five rescue, medical, and Red Cross workers on board.

# Chapter 3

The snow and freezing winds continued, as night faded and the dull grey dawn began to bleach the eastern sky. The morning's light gave the first hint of the tremendous devastation. A grimy soot-like fog filled the air and mingled with the falling snow. What the relief workers from Boston were seeing, for the first time, were the awful indications of just how powerful the explosion had been. Masses of iron, steel, broken ships, and flattened buildings, lay scattered everywhere. They had never seen anything like it.

To his great surprise, Ratshesky was advised that the Prime Minister of Canada, Sir Robert Borden was in a train-car nearby. Ratshesky asked to have a message sent, inviting the Prime Minister to join him in his car. It turns out the Prime Minister had been campaigning in Prince Edward Island when he'd heard the news about Halifax the day before and rushed to the city. When the Prime Minister was advised that the Massachusetts relief train had arrived, he immediately left his train car, and through the freshly fallen, knee-deep snow, quickly made his way over to greet them. He warmly welcomed them and told them with great sincerity how grateful he was for their quick response to the terrible tragedy.

Major Harold Giddings, who was in command of the Boston medical teams, joined Ratshesky and Borden, and the three started to make their way to Halifax City Hall, in search of Peter Martin, the mayor of Halifax. The car that transported them practically stumbled through streets filled with debris. The men looked in horror at the miles of shattered buildings. Everywhere, terror-stricken residents wandered about in a dazed state.

Major Giddings and Ratshesky had both spent the past thirty hours preparing for what was to come. They knew that, when they arrived in Halifax, their top priority would be to implement measures to ensure organization. Certainly one of the most urgent tasks would be setting up search and rescue teams to find survivors, and at the same time, setting up emergency hospitals.

These three men, and all of the rescue workers, had to keep their emotions in check in order to help in the midst of the horror. There was one sight that sent an arrow of sorrow into Ratshesky's heart. As they were riding, they saw a family dog—a brown Labrador retriever—that had somehow survived the blast. It was sitting faithfully beside the dead bodies of its beloved family, and seemed to be waiting for them to wake up. It shivered in the cold, its coat covered with thick snow. Several other frantic dogs were running through the ruins, looking for their masters. Horses wandered the streets, some still harnessed to empty, broken wagons. Ratshesky turned to Major Giddings and reminded him they would need to contact the Societies for the Prevention of Cruelty to Animals in both Canada and Massachusetts, letting them know to send emergency teams for the search and rescue of pets and livestock that had survived across the city, some of which were still trapped in the rubble.

The automobile that was dispatched to pick the men up, to take them to city hall, was driven by a quiet young man. He had been ferrying wounded citizens to hospitals and shelters for the past thirty hours. He had lost his wife and four children in the explosion. He, like all the other able-bodied survivors, had put aside his own grief, rolled up his sleeves, and joined in the desperate and heroic work of saving lives. Whatever cars or trucks survived the blast were automatically used as ambulances.

As the car pulled into the parade ground at Halifax City Hall, Ratshesky looked up at the huge clock tower. The time had stopped at 9:06 a.m.—the very moment of the explosion. It stood as a grim testament to the instant when life in the city changed forever.

Prime Minister Borden stepped out the car and walked over to the driver, gesturing for the young man to get out. "Thank you so much, son," he began. "And the good people of Canada thank you as well, and are grateful for your devotion and service during this time of need." Major Giddings stepped forward, saying, "The people of the state of Massachusetts extend their deepest sympathy for your loss, sir, and we will do everything humanly possible to help your city."

Ratshesky stepped forward and warmly shook the young driver's hand. The driver stood in the snow wearing only a thin grey coat and no gloves. Ratshesky took off his own thick wool coat and removed his leather gloves, wrapping the coat around the driver's shoulders and tucking his gloves into the pocket, telling him, "God bless you."

Just as Ratshesky, Prime Minister Borden, and Major Giddings were about to turn and enter the chaotic scene at city hall, they heard the young man say, "Please, tell the people of Boston, Massachusetts 'thank you' and tell them we will never forget their kindness in our darkest hour. Never."

# Chapter 4

The three men entered the city hall, and found chaos. The windows had been blown out, and hysterical people were begging for medical aid or food. Some begged for help rescuing their family members, still trapped, wounded, and dying in the rubble. The mayor's secretary greeted the men and led them into a twelve-by-twenty-foot room that was somewhat removed from the confusion going on everywhere else in the building. They were informed that the mayor was out of town and that Colonel McKelvie Bell and his committee were in full charge of the medical relief for the entire city. Colonel Bell looked exhausted, and like the other committee members, showed the effect of this devastating shock in his eyes. Colonel Bell extended his hand and warmly welcomed the Prime Minister and the team from Boston.

"It has become apparent," he said to them, "that a ship, the *Mont Blanc* was carrying tons of explosive material when it collided with another ship, caught fire, and then exploded. We are estimating that thousands are dead or dying, and many more thousands wounded and homeless." He looked grim. "You know, I started the first battlefield hospital in France in 1914, at the beginning of the war. I have never seen anything on the battlefront equal to the scenes of destruction here in Halifax. I have never seen injuries like this. The blast created this hurricane of broken glass, with particles flying through the air at incredible speed, as just about every window in the city blew out in seconds. We have hundreds of wounded citizens wandering helplessly around ... completely blind."

The continuing snowstorms made the search and rescue efforts both difficult and dangerous. The wreckage was freezing into solid masses, covered by ice and snow, and making it difficult for rescuers to reach victims. Ratshesky gently assured Colonel Bell that more medical help and supplies of all kinds were already on their way from Boston. Ratshesky did not want to overstep his bounds in any way, but suggested that they all find a secure building that was away from city hall and not damaged. The first thing they needed to do was sit down and make a plan to create organization for what was about to come. Relief workers, supplies, money, food, doctors, nurses, and trade workers would all be pouring into Halifax from everywhere in Canada and the United States. Continuing search and rescue efforts would coincide with the repairing of buildings suitable to be turned into hospitals, as quickly as possible.

"We have thousands of wounded soldiers," Bell said, "Who were in hospitals here, recuperating from the injuries of war. These boys, some who can barely walk at all, have given up their hospital beds for wounded civilians, and are taking care of them as well. To compound the situation, there is another ship on its way from the battlefront with 1,000 wounded Canadian soldiers expecting to be admitted into hospitals here. They have no idea what has happened." Colonel Bell's face was pale and showing his deep concern about all the wounded civilians and military men in need of urgent care. Too many doctors and nurses were either away in Europe, serving in the war, or had been killed or injured in the explosion.

"We will be ready for them," Ratshesky confidently assured Bell. "I promise you." Relief spread across Bell's face. He was feeling more confident by the hour, now that the Americans were by his side.

Earlier, the American sailors from the steamship *Old Colony* had been out to sea, heading for England, when they'd heard the enormous sound of the blast. They saw the frightening sight of a huge, towering black cloud from the explosion rising high into the sky above Halifax. The commanding officer of the *Old Colony* changed course and immediately headed toward Halifax.

"Get this ship ready to receive injured victims as soon as we enter the harbor," he said. "I don't know what has happened, but it is bad. Very bad." Approaching the harbor they were greeted by a sight on shore and in the water that looked like the end of the world. They quickly took 200 wounded citizens aboard, creating a makeshift hospital, and sent other sailors to shore to help with the cleanup of the Bellevue building, to transform it into a hospital for the American medical team. All the windows and doors had been blown out, and the floor was covered with water, ice, snow, and shattered glass. Fifty sailors from the *Old Colony* began working tirelessly, beside Canadian soldiers who were stationed in Halifax at the time of the explosion. They covered open windows, cleaned debris, and scrubbed floors.

The Story of the 1917 Halifax Explosion and the Boston Tree

The American Bellevue Hospital was up and running within hours.

# Chapter 5

Abraham Ratshesky and the team from the Massachusetts Halifax Relief Expedition worked fearlessly around the clock, barely taking time to eat or sleep for days on end, heroically saving lives and creating order out of a chaotic and desperate situation. The press corps, which had travelled on the Massachusetts-Halifax Relief Expedition train, reported daily on the unimaginable destruction and desperation of the city. Their reporting of the countless heartbreaking stories of human tragedy ultimately went around the world. Their heroic reporting was critical in raising an enormous outpouring of additional aid from other government organizations, as well as private citizens and businesses across the United States and the world.

The exhausted and traumatized Canadian medical personnel, rescue workers, civilians, and soldiers who stood alone for those first thirty hours after the blast would never forget the kind, strong, steady, and selfless help their American neighbors had extended to them.

By December 14, the Americans needed to return to Boston to attend to their duties following the recent US entry into the Great War. They had accomplished what they had intended to do, and everything was in place, carefully planned, organized, and self-sufficiently operating. It was now ready to be handed over and run smoothly without them.

# Epilogue

The day before the Massachusetts-Halifax Relief Expedition returned to Boston, doctors Major Baker, Captain Nathaniel Morse, and Captain Lapham all dressed up as Santa Claus and delivered toys, which had been donated from across Canada and the United States, to the injured children in hospital.

Governor McCall, the state of Massachusetts, the city of Boston, and Abraham Ratshesky continued offering their assistance to the stricken city for many months following the disaster, by building housing for the homeless, reconstructing neighborhoods that were destroyed, and offering financial aid. This was a magnificent humanitarian and noble mission, never forgotten by Nova Scotians and Canadians alike.

Christmas trees are an ancient symbol of hope and rebirth, and their shining lights are a symbol of light in the darkness. And this is what the good people of Boston and Massachusetts gave to the survivors of the Halifax Explosion: hope ... and a light in the darkness of their despair. The gift of Christmas tree to the people of Boston is the perfect symbolic gesture of thanks.

# "We Will See You Through"

Composers: Mark Despault, Tom Leighton, and Suzanne Pasternak
Arrangement: Tom Leighton
The Sheet Music Story and Lyrics

Digby, Nova Scotia native Mark Despault composed this beautiful and haunting song several years ago. In 2015, Tom Leighton and I expanded the song musically and lyrically. Tom then arranged for it to be performed by the Boston Children's Choir and the Nova Scotia Mass Choir during tree ceremonies in Halifax and Boston. It was performed by the Nova Scotia Mass Choir and filmed in Halifax that same year. Then it was aired at the Boston-tree lighting in front of an audience of 30,000 in person, and 300,000 watching on television.

We were all delighted to learn that a hundred and thirty young school children had also lined the street of Truro, Nova Scotia to sing "We Will See You Through" as the tree passed through town.

This song specifically speaks to the enduring friendship between the United States and Canada. Without question or hesitation, these two countries respond in times of crisis, offering each other whatever resources and help is required. This has been proven time and time again in recent memory. During 9/11, many American airplanes emergency landed in Canadian airports. Canadian electrical workers and trucks rushed to New York and New Jersey in the aftermath of hurricane Sandy. American's offered helping hands when a devastating ice-storm caused electrical outages across Ontario and Quebec. In the winter of 2015, a caravan of New York State Troopers rescued a bus load of Canadians who were trapped during a vicious blizzard outside of Buffalo, New York, and drove them over the border into Canada. The relationship between our two countries is a shining example of international relations, and this song is a sincere and heartfelt tribute to these two great countries:

# *Lyrics*

When your life grows cold and darkness has come over you

And everything is lost and there's no hope in sight

And blackness fills the sky and the sun no longer shines for you

You are not alone; we will see you through

We will see you through; your story is not over now

You will rise again, as sure as life goes on

You will feel the strength flowing back inside of you

You are not alone; we will see you through

If the sky should fall and the earth beneath your feet should knock you to your knees

We are there by your side, always there by your side

With helping hands across our border

You are not alone; we will see you through

Recording is available on

https://open.spotify.com/trac/6y86yrQoElaT7ulmsN1gee

https://itun.es/ca/m01-gb

CD Baby and Amazon

## We Will See You Through

Suzanne Pasternak

revised Oct 15/'16

by S. Pasternak, M. Despault, & T. Leighton ©2014

When your life grows cold and dark-ness has come o-ver you and ev-'ry-thing is lost and there's no hope in sight. and black-ness fills the sky. The sun no long-er shines for you, you are not a-lone, we will see you through. We will see you through, your stor-y is not o - - ver now, you will rise a-gain as sure as life goes on. You will feel the strength flow-ing back in-side of you, you are not a-lone, We will see you through. Ooo If the sky should fall and the earth be-neath your feet should

# The Story of the 1917 Halifax Explosion and the Boston Tree

*We Will See You Through*

knock you to your knees. We are there by your side, Al-ways there by your side, with help-ing hands a cross our bor- der. We will see you through, your stor-y is not o - - - ver now, you will rise a - gain as sure as life goes on. You will feel the strength flow-ing back in - side of you, you are not a - lone, We'll be there with you, you are not a - lone, We will see you through. We will see you through. We will see you through.

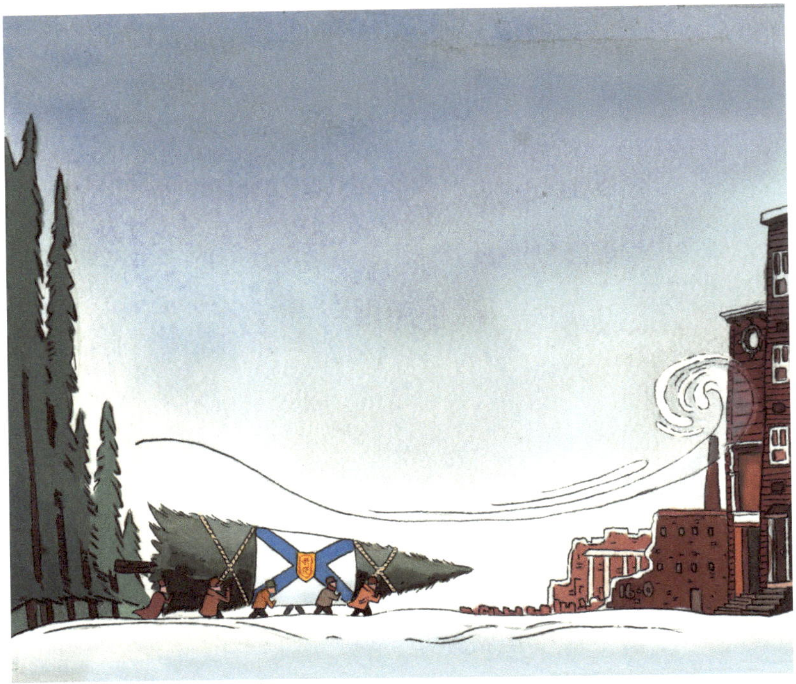

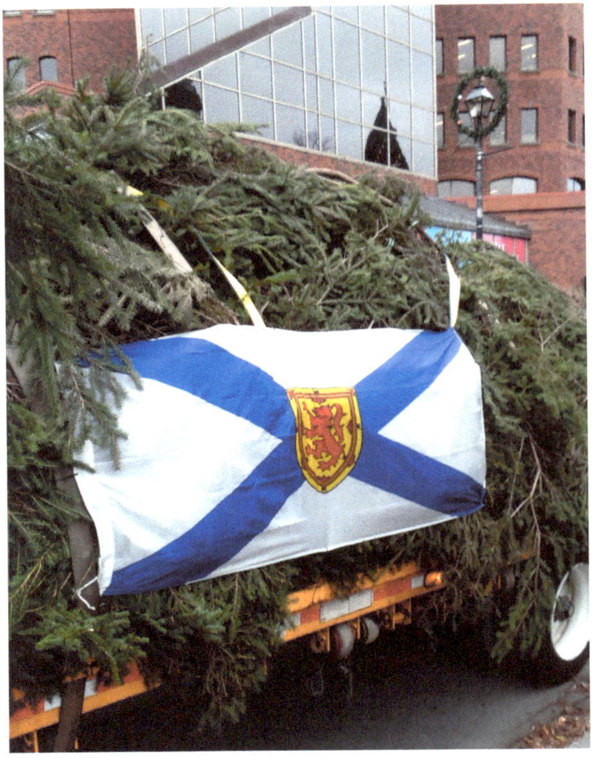

# *Additional Resources*

Books

*Mahar, James; Mahar, Rowena (1998). Too Many To Mourn – One Family's Tragedy in the Halifax Explosion. Nimbus Publishing. ISBN 978-1-55109-240-9.*

*Kitz, Janet (1992). The Survivors: The Children of the Halifax Explosion. Nimbus Publishing.*

*Glasner, Joyce (2003). The Halifax Explosion: Surviving the Blast that Shook a Nation. Altitude Press. ISBN 978-1-55153-942-3.*

*Beed, Blair (2002). 1917 Halifax Explosion and American Response (2nd ed.). Dtours Visitors and Convention Service. ISBN 0-9684383-1-8.*

*Gilligan, Edmund (February 1938). "Death in Halifax". American Mercury.* **43** *(170): 175–181.*

World Wide Web

Halifax Public Library - http://www.halifaxpubliclibraries.ca/research/topics/local-history-genealogy/halifax-explosion-links.html

Flickr photos of relief effort from Massachusetts Library - https://www.flickr.com/photos/mastatelibrary/sets/72157638350026413/

The Maritime Museum of the Atlantic Halifax Explosion web page

*"Just One Big Mess": The Halifax Explosion, 1917* NFB documentary.

CBC Halifax Explosion Web Site: a large interactive web site about the explosion

Information and video of survivors - http://www.cbc.ca/news/canada/nova-scotia/halifax-explosion-canadian-national-institute-for-the-blind-imo-mont-blanc-1.3878921

A heartfelt correspondence between the cities - http://www.halifax.ca/archives/HalifaxThanksBostonforExplosionRelief1918.php

CPSIA information can be obtained
at www.ICGtesting.com
Printed in the USA
BVHW020601301118
534413BV00009BA/44/P